A Convergence of Unanticipated Consequences

Russ Messing

DEERGNAW PRESS

Acknowledgements

To the editors of the following publications in which some of these poems in earlier forms have appeared: *Footnotes*, *Hair Pieces*, and *Handwriting*.

To Margaret Shapiro, whose dedication, support, enthusiasm, and plain hard work has inspired so many. To the writers in our groups: Thanks for making it all safe and for the courage to keep on.

To Francesca Preston who has guided me with gentle suggestions, unerring accuracy, and disarming honesty. Her sense of harmony and beauty, her knowledge and intuition, and her willingness to embrace my quirkiness has made this experience and this collection all the better.

To Jason Hill, who has helped guide me through the maze with patience and a smile.

To my friends, who listen and support, and to the writers at the Healdsburg Literary Guild who love the word and write because they have to.

To Jeanne, Ali, and Jake, who support their papa and his dreams; who live and manifest their own dreams; who feel my deep love, and have the grace to smile when I toast them and cry.

To Arlene who always wants to hear the next poem, who creates beauty and poetry in and of our lives, who walks with me down our winding, mostly sun-drenched path.

Table of Contents

One

Two

Three

Four

Five

Six

Dedicated to Arlene,
my beloved,
who lightens the load
and lights up my life.

In beauty.

Apple

After a bite from a sweet red apple,
lo and behold, my teeth uncovered
the back of a nude—a woman for sure!

There was her right shoulder, then a back with
swooping spine, the inward curve of a waist,
and the unmistakable bloom of full, soft bottom.

The rest of her stayed hidden beneath
that curtain of dark crimson and it seemed she
might be in prayer, kneeling before an altar.

Was she sitting cross-legged, I wondered,
waiting for a sign or the sun, maybe her lover?
Her head, surely it was bowed, perhaps in worship.

Then, somehow, I knew it was morning,
that Buddha-style and naked she was on her bed,
the sheets all a-crumple, hands on her belly.

The sun had risen, the breeze from the open window
brushed the down on her neck, and with eyes closed
she mistook my breathing for the slight, warm wind.

Although I thought to nibble more, to uncover
the curve of her breast, the cradle of a lap,
I let her be, safe inside the apple of the morning.

The Back of an Envelope

He had never written a poem on the back of an envelope

and wondered if it was bad form or just laziness.

He felt lonely there in the blue kitchen, only the cockatiel,

some cobwebs, and the fridge's hum filling up the room.

Of course, the insurance company that sent him their statement

doesn't give a damn about the envelope, they just want their money.

Yet he couldn't help but feel his father glowering over him

tsk-tsking, telling him to get a proper piece of clean paper,

when what he was really thinking is that poetry is for sissy boys

and what he *wasn't* saying is: Son, you won't amount to anything.

I Love the Names of Birds

I love the names of birds:
the White-collared Swift, the Greylag Goose,
the Frigate Bird and Blue-footed Booby, and
for sure, the Rufous-rumped Antwren.

The names, they tell me something,
more than just a hint, they add some spice,
shout out color, shape, home or trait;
give me a place to come home to.

I've always believed in magic:
when the silver coins disappear,
how the spangled woman is cut in half,
that the birds return every year.

I'd like to think those Red-winged Blackbirds,
whose "conk-a-reeeee" I've come to love, but
no longer hear in our round-pond reeds,
have found another home, not just up and died.

But maybe they're still here, like always,
only now with a brand new name—
say, the Black-throated Dreamcatcher—
and I haven't heard or seen them
because no one's told me of the changes.

Libido

My libido's just sitting there in the fridge
on the second shelf wedged between
some kalamatas and a half carafe of flat vin blanc.

The good news: it's keeping,
though its usual brilliant red is clearly fading.
The bad news: it's cold, almost gelatinous,
and looking—shall I say?—spent.

So I pull it out and set it on the ledge behind the sink,
hoping for a thaw. But the day turns gray
and the rains come hard, bring on night, and I forget.

Only later, piss time, 2 a.m., do I remember
and slump downstairs naked to stash it again
in the fridge, and—thinking it might be more comfortable
with things I'd laid my hands on—set it between the dill pickles
I put up last summer and my delicious
home-made-mucho-garlic pesto.

By morning its half-remembered crimson
is rust-colored and it's clear that
cold isn't working, so, tired of being a guy,
I ask my wife what to do.

She smiles, crooks her finger, then points to the stairs.
I nod and start on up. But as I do, I glimpse her
holding it gingerly, like she did with our parakeet,
Slim, after he'd broken his leg and she'd fixed it with a splint.

Cold Toes

What I bring with me today are my ice-cold toes—
ten small sausages kept in the freezer,
brought out too late for breakfast's thawing.

They sit locked and numb, stiff in my socks, on strike.
Not feeling, they thumb their toe-noses, mock the socks,
snicker at my lame attempts at warming.

It's like they're disembodied, mysterious creatures
mistakenly attached to me and ticked off about it,
like spoiled children dedicated to torment and taunt.

When I listen closely I even hear their snivels, their sniggers:
"Chill out." "Grin and bear it." "Hang in there, wuss," they sneer.
They're bullies, smug and pompous. Ignoring doesn't help.

So, I toast them up as best I can—right now, in fact—
imagining myself on a beach, basting in the warm breeze,
winter heat—Hawaii, mid-afternoon, sweat, salt, sun.

A woman bikinis by, sees my toes all a-wiggle, smiles,
sashays on. They smile back in warm response
like children do when hugged, snuggling into down.

I watch her way too long, forget about the toes.
They're pissed, miss the babe, the sound of waves,
the grit of sand. They start to throb again, cold, cold, cold.

It's then I hear them snicker, cackle as one, like a witch,
pleased as ice-cold punch to rule the roost from bottom up,
the way the meek might be in triumph or the Fool is with the King.

Makeover

She would like to lose her waddle,
wished her wattle wouldn't wobble,
and her belly stop its jiggle.
So, instead of morning bagel
she sips her tea, something floral,
and for lunch just plain and simple.
Then to the gym for the treadmill,
modest weights for glutes and pectorals,
then some crunches for abdominals.
It's a total re-do, all essential,
once political, now is personal.
No more wiggles, no more wattle;
no more meatballs, no more waffles;
no more girdles, bye-bye jiggle;
gone love handles and their struggles.
Now her world is one big bauble,
Look, she glitters! How she dazzles!
Now clap your hands and wait for trouble...

Like Any Good Poet

Like any good poet worth his salt
I have taken myself outside on
this idyllic spring day carrying
only a pen, my writing book,
some intention, and a glass of wine.

Poets love days like this and to help me along
it would be good to know the names of these
nickel-sized pinkish flowers, as well as know why
one bee goes to them while another prefers
diving into the lavender wisteria.

And to better describe this perfect day
with a metaphor or two, I could also stand
to be versed in a number of pagan or
Christian reasons for May Day (which
I've forgotten to mention is this very day).

I should also tell you that some unseen bird
just now barely missed my balding pate
with an ill-aimed dropping, as that might provide
an amusing counterpoint for my elegy to spring
which may gush out and flow in any moment.

But that would require me to actually open
this book, take the Bic from my plaid shirt pocket,
set down this brilliant Ruben-esque zin,
and stop my magical thinking that this pen
is a wizard and that words have wings.

Partial Knee Replacement

This morning on the radio I heard
an ad for a partial knee replacement
and wondered why bother with a full knee
when a partial one will fill the bill?

Like my grandma did, I asked myself:
My word, what is this world coming to?
It's not like knees are hot sellers, and, oh lord,
how many folk even need a partial knee?

Why not ads for three-legged cats,
spent calla lilies, or vacations in Duluth?
What about spots for used galoshes,
maybe pubic hair weaving, holey socks.

I wonder if digital this and dot.com that
have left me behind, a toothless saw
propped against a shabby, gray shed,
curving in on myself, useless but content.

I shake my head, head for the local coffee shop—
just a plain old cup of joe please, no espresso,
a little room for cream, thank you, and a plain
old-fashioned donut, not some yuppy scone—

to breathe in the hum of the crew-cut cops,
the four orange-shirted city workers trading jibes,
the five Bible ladies cozied in with Jesus,
and smile, knowing we all have our knees about us.

Some Last Things

Some last things I want to tell you:

I won't take the poison under the sink.
I think that's yours to deal with.

But I will take the chamois cloth you gave me,
the special one, you said, just for the piano keys.

And my scissors, too, which you always borrow
and your ankle bracelet which I snipped off last night.

Notice, please, I've swept the cat hairs from the couch
so you may think kindly of me from time to time.

The kitchen clock I leave with you
as time will go slowly enough, I fear.

I want the photo of us in the hammock,
still wondering who took it since we were alone.

I'll take my clothes to save you a Goodwill trip,
but leave my Boy Scout medals as counterpoints.

I'll keep your smell in my waterproof tin
to kindle memory in case of emergency.

You can keep all your plans and lists.
There's just no need to make you muddled.

A few last things to know: I love you. Forget about the hurts,
I'll take them off your hands. The keys are in the freezer.

Two

On the Balcony

Prince William kisses Kate.
I wouldn't call it a sexy kiss
or passionate, no, more like
obligatory, though with sweetness.
Sure, I know it's not decorous
to wonder about their sex life,
but I just can't help it,
their plumbing being the same as ours.

Her thin lips, his slight paunch—
oh, I know I'm being picky—
but when they get back to their
castle do they tear off their clothes,
dance naked in the moonlight?
Do they coo, hum, giggle, moan?
Does she shriek like a siren?
Does he bellow like a bull?

They seem so prim and proper
like royals ought to be,
but maybe, just perchance,
they jump, jump, jump on their royal bed,
her slight tits, his royal balls
jouncing and a-bouncing
with nary a trace of
pomp and circumstance.

Getting Down

To get close to a giant tortoise
you have to get down on your belly,
eye to eye, inch your way forward
like a soldier in a movie,
let her see you're no threat,
let her know you're mildly interested,
like you would be wooing a woman.

Better to be a ground finch, hop in front
to show you're ready, then be welcomed
to peck at parasites and dine on ticks
from her age-old skin and outstretched neck.
To be her friend, to sing, "Let's take a stroll
down the track to the rain-filled pool."

Or better still, be a tortoise too, bob your head,
and bluster, grunt, stamp your feet;
next, stretch your neck and circle 'round
to feel the wet earth brush your husk,
then bite her neck and ram her shell.

But, alas, I'm not. I'm just a guy.
So the next best thing, like I said,
is to get on down, breathe real slow,
and pretend I have my own thick shell to hide in.

Fresh

If I were homeless I'd get me to Sal's
for some clean clothes and head to
Fresh Choice with the eight dollars
I begged at the end of the freeway ramp.

Then I'd start with, I mean, load up
the tray with two salads for today.
I'd sit in the back where the fewest
people go, and after the salads
I'd slide back in line and load up,
really pile on those little baked potatoes
all wrapped in tinfoil, some pizza slices,
hot rolls and muffins, butter.

Then like a crafty bandit, tuck it all
in the coves of my trusty daypack.

I'd get me a fruit plate, chew slow
like a Buddha-guy, tastes bursting sweet
on my tongue, down my throat.
I'd grin a lot, nod at the busboy,
pocket a knife and fork, plate some
triple-decadence chocolate brownies, those
zucchini and carrot clove-spiced cupcakes,
wrap 'em in napkins.

Then snuggle it all down into
the corners of my trusty daypack.

I'd be my own Santa Claus, good fairy,
and Snow White rolled into one.
I'd waddle out like the Goodyear blimp,
a big shine spread over my face,
thinking of the feast tonight,
maybe who I'd share it with,
whistling my way out like I just won
the jackpot, feeling full and fresh.

A Hard Rain

"A hard rain is gonna fall," rasped Dylan.
He was right, maybe sixteen inches.
"You guys still there?" people emailed.

Yeah, except that our canoe filled with water
and bubbled down to the bottom of the pond
while our paddles, via some great plan,
stood at attention in the storage locker in town;

Except that our life vests were riddled with
mouse tunnels and our recently re-roofed roof
leaked in six places and the drip-drip-drip
into six revolving pots drove us crazy;

Except that we lost electricity for three days,
the ice cream ran like goo,
the beans sprouted green coats,
and the milk smelled rank as puke.

As the water rose higher and higher,
I swear, a large wooden boat with animals craning
from all its portholes and decks drew closer
and between the lightning cracks and thunder drones
we heard some very important voice booming
"Repent," or "Relent," or Free Rent."
It was hard to tell.

So we did the only sane thing left:
climbed into bed, lit some candles,
spread the tan afghan over the covers,
and made love more than you need to know.

Scorcher

Your bro, plus Lolo and Leeny
stomped by yesterday—surprise—
rockets in their jeans, beads in their hair
sportin' sass and whatchoo mean.

Me, curled up on the hide-a-bed
doing nothing 'cept waiting for dark,
no interest in this or that, their snarky talk.
doin' nothing, just stayin' cool.

Kicking back, I tell them. Leave me be.
Surprise, surprise, not a word of shit, but
they do that stupid one shoulder shrug
with the lips all puckered like on YouTube.

And Leeny, she gives me that tired old sex pout
like I'm gonna be missing out on something good,
but I just turn the cheek, like the Bible sez.
Good riddance, I say. It's too damn hot to be cool.

Forgotten Bread

The mouse's unlucky night
began as usual: a stretch,
a yawn, another stretch,
then a tour 'round the nest,
a quick sprucing up.

Then out the split
in the silver insulation,
past the chink
in the wallboard, through
the hole in the corner.

There he stopped, sniffed,
took two cautious steps
into the kitchen, inched
his circuit along the edges
doing due diligence.

Finally there in the corner
by the stove a crumb
of forgotten bread and further
a sliver of almond and—at last—
the slinky pull of peanut butter.

But sometimes things *are*
too good to be true:
think Trojan horse,
the deft sleight of hand,
that transvestite whore, or
your mirror's slippery whisper.

Thwack!

Happy Flock

I don't understand birders,
how they coo and crow
at the sighting of their
thirteenth warbler finch,
their umpteenth blue-footed booby,
yet another flightless cormorant.

Every night they gather,
swarming over h'or d'oeuvres,
nibbling on the day's sightings.
"Green-billed flimsy," one hoots.
"Check!" others cluck.
"Where?" a few will squawk.

Like penguins honking and hawing
they puff up and crane their necks,
a happy flock circling round and round
alighting on a single crumb or morsel.
I cannot sniff out envy, nor despair,
not even one flicker of competition.

No, it's more genuine, like your
warm slippers when my feet are cold.
I wish I had them, but I'm glad for you.
Which is how I felt just then,
wishing I had spotted the lava heron,
that I, too, had such soaring passion.

Three

Numbsuit

Today I went to the mall to buy a Numbsuit,
you know, the one they advertise on the internet.
I chose the Classic Cut, the gray one, with no cuffs
to catch dropped feelings, and the pockets sewn shut
to keep out memories, excitement, old hopes.

Next, a slow walk over to the costume store
to buy the "Plain Man" mask, the one with those
ineffable lips, no smile or frown, pale skin, blank eye holes.
After that to the video store to rent the saddest movies,
then two doors down to the drug store for a hand mirror.

Tonight I'll practice, sit and watch *Sophie's Choice*,
stare at myself and keep my face still like stone.
I'll clean my cuticles, practice boredom, be a clam.
I will yawn like old men do at weddings or wakes,
as if nothing's new, like there's nowhere else to go.

But now I am sitting in the park, my Numbsuit on,
watching a dog knock a boy into the fountain.
The kid screams, his mother drops his root-beer float
on her white jeans, rushes to swoop him from harm.
(Her shirt clings, her nipples poke through.)

I take inventory: No compassion or lusting.
No pull to comfort or move to help. Not even caring.
Just a feeble lean forward, one knee bending,
as if I had thought to lend a hand. But I catch myself,
get up and leave, Numbsuit dry and wrinkle-free.

Cross Words

Yesterday I tossed my cell phone in the pool
watched its small delicate splash, the bare ripples,
and slow weaving descent to the bottom where it
settled soft, black against blue.

I thought it might have finally reached a place of peace,
all its bells and apps at last asleep, glubbingly giving thanks
that there was no more need to remind me of a birthday,
help me waste my time, tell me the answer.

I imagined there being one final electric gurgle, one last
email which no one would ever get, one wet word puzzle
letting me know our time together had been a pleasure,
even though I was a slow and fumbling luddite.

Later, in bed doing the Sunday crossword, I came to 1-Down:
"Something always needed" and thought of my old phone,
now in sodden peace, submerged in ten feet of chlorinated water.
Goodbye, I whispered, wondering who I was talking to.

Finally, puzzle finished, just as I was nodding off,
I thought I heard a sound, faint as old grief,
some whoosh like birds make when they leave,
like lovers do when there's nothing more to say.

Auditions

You'll be pissed off when you're gone and dead—
eternity on your empty hands filled with
pink-cheeked angels, their sappy music.
Or if it's hell, too damn much heat,
moans and screams, that Bosch-y buggering.

But heaven, hell, or in between
there'll be no one to brood for or yell at,
no one to run from, ignore, or slam.
Holier than thou will be out of the question,
while sulks and snubs will get you judged.

Grumbling won't get you far, nor will pouting.
Being an apprentice angel holds no lure—
lyres and smiles, awkward wings, adore, adore, adore!
While the thought of trying out for the Devil
sounds like horror, some infernal torture.

What about one climate always spring,
the other brimstone with brine as drink?
But, of this I'm sure: that skinned alive
or dodging wings bring on too much time
to relive the life you either wasted or defiled.

I-Brain

I'm all a-jangle, so I flip on my I-Brain,
do a quick turn through all the applications,
find "BuzzTimeTrivia," "BrainBuster," "Butt Jokes,"
"Noontime Fantasies"—all my favorites.

But I'm in no mood for brain caffeine.
I'm wanting soothing: something like "DreamStreet,"
that app that flattens time, binds left brain and right,
like Ecstasy did, like hammocks do.

Last night was too charged—fights with the wife,
about my dishes undone, not enough sex—
and I tap-tap-tap right into "DreamStreet,"
watch my I-Brain scroll through "Mountain Stream,"
then "Summer Drizzle," past "Big Sur Wave Break"—
all so sixties, so cliché, but why not, I think,
why not trip on back to them good old days?

I fix on "Here, Now" and all that's there is me:
blue-green eyes, sly grin, my big nose, pink skin,
grey beard, thinning lips, and I zoom in more
into the scars and pores, the vessels and capillaries,
the veins, their molecules and atoms, 'til I come to rest
in some slow universe of greens and blues and reds
where there is nothing but a cresting hum that ebbs,
then grows, then ebbs again like breath,

like the sea or years, like love does, maybe death.

Hosting

My calves are infested by Martians, maybe Venusians,
who are either in great ecstasy, dancing madly
on the wires of my veins, and somersaulting like
angels do, reveling in the curtains of this world, or

in great distress, clamoring for release from this prison
of skin, blood, and muscle, pushing their airy bodies
with every one of their twenty-seven extremities in
unimaginable double and tumble-jointed ways.

I place one ankle on my opposite knee and let
my calf muscle dangle, watch in wonder the mash
of slides and skitters, the ups and downs,
across the now-wrinkled, almost hairless skin.

I might do this for hours with the barest of hopes that
at any moment a pore will stretch and groan and out will squeeze
a head, an arm, some unknown body part, a crop of hair;
maybe even an energy bolt, a flash of time, the smell of kelp.

I'll stay still, still as stone, 'til they all have squiggled out,
then say in the calmest of tones, like a holy man might,
"Welcome. I've waited eternities for this moment.
But at the risk of being rude, what took you so long?"

Emptying the Hands

My hands are stuffed like a hoarder's house,
filled with toys broken and new, crates of cloth, tools,
burnt out Christmas lights, stacks of books, old dreams.

I want to empty it all, start all over,
call in the junk trucks, the organizers, the shrinks,
the shredders, and the barrow wheelers.

But I am stuck in some land of cold schemes with
lonely plans, pinioned under hope piles, old files,
dirty dishes, empty boxes, strewn and rancid dreams.

Oh, yeh, I say, someday I'll make that box
to hold these strong toy soldiers, and someday I'll
fix the faucets, do the photo albums for the kids.

But my hands are too full, holding onto maybe and when,
to what if and someday, to I want to remember.
My fingers feel fisted shut, tight like a miser's mouth.

Maybe tomorrow, maybe when I wake up tomorrow...
if it's sunny and I can find some empty boxes, some tape.
If only I can find some time, some tape, some boxes.

Sour-Pussing

Since my mother died, I've lost my smile,
retraced my steps, looked in all the usual places:
asked at the bank, the coffee shop, the p.o., and the park.
It's not under the car or in it, not beside the bed or on it.
I'm at a loss and comedy doesn't help. My jowls hang limp.

It's hard not having your smile, makes you want to hide,
walk with your head down, pretend you're important.
I've tried staying home to stand before the mirror,
thinking if I stare hard enough it'll pop out,
But it doesn't work. My cheeks hang loose and I flit on by.

So instead I close my eyes, see me with her smile on,
and for the briefest of blinks the ends of my lips curl upward.
Like working out, I practice every day to get it stronger.
And every little bit I hear my mother say, "I'm dead already.
All this sour-pussing ain't gonna bring me back. Get over it."

Four

When Saturn Comes to Call

When Saturn comes to my garden he hovers like fog,
spits on the zucchini and shrinks the grapes.
Tomatoes don't ripen. The onions arrive soft and rotten.
Ripped husks of corn drip pale, shriveled kernels.

I have sung incantations, built a scarecrow named Zeus.
I have put up a maypole and danced around it naked,
weaving silken ribbons into a giant phallus.
I have called on the Virgin, the Whore, and the Sirens.

But Saturn slavers on, froth dripping from his maw
as he spoils the apples, melts the thorns on the blackberries,
turns the pumpkins to ash. He has split the melons
and soured the plums. The scorched pears are beyond salvation,
mushy and impotent as old men.

I have read the horoscope, gone to Mass,
liberated the prayer rug from the basement.
I have planted clover, nailed a horseshoe to the barn.
I have crossed my fingers, prayed, splayed myself humble.
But Saturn has his way, bile and spittle, spittle and bile,
and I shuffle off, a tired old man, bent-backed and beaten.

A Roomful of Birders

Whenever she makes a point
the woman with the bouffant hair-do,
the one with everything in place,
flings her fingers out—a señorita and her fan.
She sounds a three-note giggle,
ducks her head three times fast, then
swallows hard waiting for an answer.

She introduces herself, martini in hand.
The room banter is loud and I think she says,
"Hi, I'm Robin." "Robin?" I ask, not sure.
She grins, head-a-bob like pecking for worms.
"An easy mnemonic," I joke above the noise.
"Don't I know. Don't I know," she two-time trills.
I'd like to twitter back, but have no clue.

She is bending forward into her drink
as if sniffing when a real birder inches in,
bends forward himself sipping glances
from her modest bodice, her tempting breasts
drawing him in—the way, one park ranger said,
the female brown finch does just before mating.
Then, right on cue, they cock their heads
and I hear her sing, like the Simple-billed Tingler,

Tee-hee, tee-hee, tit-tit, tee-hee.

Sitting Vigil With Mom

I. "You have lots of teeth," she whispers.
   She has lost words, this time *smile*.
   We nod, show off our pearly whites.
   The blue of her eyes is paler now,
   though still they shine, Mom's old deep song.
   Oxygen in, catheter out, love all around.
   All our focus on her comfort, all of hers
   on holding on. May death come softly.

II. Part of me is dying with her.
    I want a magic wand to make time
    turn backwards. I have no teeth for this.
    All I've got are words: *banal* is one,
    amen another. What about *damn* and
    how about *thanks*? I like *blessed* as in
    blessed be. I think *tender*, too,
    which makes me grin, have teeth.

III. Ten inches of snow. Blankets of
     white on the ground, on her bed too,
     all sound muffled save each exhale
     she moans. No ivories now. We hope it's
     not pain. Muted, we wonder what to do—
     so make a circle holding hands.
     Dim eyes glaze open. "I see you."
     What can we do but laugh? She beams.
     So many teeth all around. Then, that's all.

Reunion

I am perched on a wide headstone, four feet up,
knees pulled to chin, peering down at six graves:
the family plot—grandparents, parents,
my younger sister, my first son.

It is hot, late afternoon, cars rushing past,
lives in motion, while here all's at rest.
Cicadas buzz—an over-drone to traffic—
and the cemetery lawnmower hums.

I have wedged a penny beside each
stone, down where earth meets air,
while someone has left a pebble
on the family's granite marker.

Breathing slow, I let go my shoulders,
say "Hi", and wait for I don't know what.
Underground and above it, too, we
seven meet, in some fuzzy undulation.

I put down my ham and cheese sandwich,
take a sip of soda to slow things up,
think I should have brought some to share,
like any good guest would have done.

It'd be good to start a conversation,
but I'd have to make up all the parts...
so I turn to monologues: stuff about the kids,
my job, that I'm still in love, how I miss each of them.

But it's not enough. I want more and ask:
What's it like down/over/up there?
Are the stories true? Then, yow! a whir,
a shuffling, a breaking through, some low-throat "Hi's."

There, that's better. They wait their turn
like I was taught, sitting at the table,
third on the totem pole, chewing with my mouth closed,
biding time, like they do now, no place to go.

Someday I hope someone will sit over me,
another link in this chain, maybe bring a penny,
tuck it down on top, then bring me up to speed,
tell me a joke or two, then wait for me to tell one back.

Wood Gathering

At first light, stepping out slow, heading towards our old shed
to load the wheelbarrow for today's wood-stove fires
I see time hanging by a thread, swaying ever so lightly.
I take it as an omen and imagine seconds vanishing
with each piece of oak and madrone I lift and toss.

Thunk and thud every log, whirr and spin each second.
I'm not nearly ready I say to no one. *Let me be.*
This load is heavy, the tire going flat, but it's downhill
from the shed. I prop the screen door open with a log,
for some reason in a whirl, the strand swaying faster.

To keep the rug clean I make a a newspaper path to the stove.
Armload after armload I fill the hearth. I'm in a hurry,
as if a despot taking notes has filled up the ledger's last page.
Later, the fire going, my coffee ready, I remember the thread,
peek out. Now there's a second one, swinging from the mock plum.

It's silver too and flits in this morning's fog like just-lost thoughts.
Wait! On the grape vine that frames the porch, still one more!
Not yet. Will they cocoon the house in slim gauze strips?
Stop for Christ's sake! But, time—hang, sway, tock and tick—
hisses and spits, crackles. I spin to the stove, lay on more wood.

Crossroads

At some crossroads
where your throat hurts
from thinking too much
not saying enough,

where down in the bushes
a chipped cup of coffee
stains a still-sealed envelope.
Denise, it says, no address,

and draped on the fencepost
a frayed cowboy shirt still buttoned
balances on top of a hairbrush,
blond hair blowing west.

C'mon, you need some purpose!
Go ahead! Just open the damn
envelope, maybe follow the wind.
Please, you think, give me a hint!

But it's all a crock:
this crossroads, the sad shrug
to meaning-making, the way
the wind's not pointing anywhere

the way I make it up
as I go along

In Retreat

I'm going backwards, my mind
on slow slog back to lost barracks,
taking marching orders
from a blind martinet.

I'm heading backwards,
my compass stuck on south,
in retreat to some foxhole deep
behind lines I cannot find.

My fatigues fill with lists,
these boots slip, caked with glum,
while old maps and elevations
fade away, now lost in fog.

My fingers numb, I struggle on,
hold memories close, lose my way,
and wonder if I'll ever stumble back
to those safe and snug old front lines.

Friends

"I wouldn't go that far to get laid."
Pause..."Well, maybe I would."
One paints, the other writes.

Pen scratching, paint daubing.
Mostly silence, a word or two.
Two cups of tea growing cold.

These are the lines of friendship:
oil on a canvas, ink on the page,
their wrinkled tales and retold skin.

Five

Italian Lesson

Yesterday I learned a new word:
Furgone (foor-go-nay) which means truck,
like this one—white and weed-choked—left behind,
I'm guessing, right where it stopped.

Col d'Elsa sits stark in the distance,
its towers sifting through Tuscan haze.
The day is late, dust-glazed, too hot.
There is no wind. Nothing moves.

I think of a father and his son,
sweat-soaked and cursing, done,
leaving their *furgone* behind with a pat,
a sad *ciao* to an old, dead friend.

Strange how this one new word
brings such simple pleasure,
like day's end, a cold glass of water,
how it flows smooth off the tongue.

They may have passed this low stone wall,
these ragged rows of olive trees,
crossed their new-mown field, now gold,
and headed home, but on foot, bent older.

I sit shaded, roll *furgone* slowly
'round my mouth—loving its sound—
and remember when I've said goodbye.
wheeling away, my arm out the window, waving.

Question Marks

Looking in the mirror tonight
I notice on both of my ear lobes
a fine line running diagonally down and away
from my well-worn, wandering face.

They're twins I've never seen before,
newly spawned by aging, I suppose.
They're not all that troubling, really nothing,
I tell myself, watching my nose grow longer.

Funny how they look like question marks:
the fleshy lobes the points at the bottom,
the half-curled arcs being the sweep and drop—
two sudden, sloppy interrogatives.

Maybe they presage something monumental
like me winning the ne'er-to-work-again lottery,
or finally having my first menage-a-trois.
Or maybe it's bad, something cold like death.

I mean, you expect your balls to hang lower,
and you know lost keys to be part of the deal,
not to mention lost names, soft hard-ons,
errant farts, forgotten appointments.

But strangely lined ear lobes? Aarrggh!
I'm driving myself dumb and crazy.
So I take a breath like a lama might,
exhale invention, then amble off tired
to my mirror-less, mindless resting place.

For the Duration

Socked in and cabin-bound on the Mendocino coast
at the edge of a stern bluff three hundred feet
above the sea, we watch the grain-hard rain pellet
the redwood deck and hear the green-gray sea bleat
against the unseen beach below, the sky so flat,
stolid, pouting, and hunkered down, holding fast.

We are here for the duration, each a tourist
in the lands of Nowhere to Go and Ocean Beat.
Did you read about?...she asks. We sip our tea.
The sliding door is cracked. I lean back towards heat.
She's a Viking. And, me? A wimp with ice-cold feet.
So I cup them in my hands like a mother might.

Sometimes she's the teacher and I'm the taught,
other times it's just the opposite, but we coast
on through, take three left turns to make a right,
bump up against each other, doing our best—
each a guest in the other's world, each a generous host,
like sea, sky, and shore are wont to be when they meet.

Fall

She was fourteen, riding with two friends.
Sunday. Ten o'clock in October fields.
The sun still low in the sky, cornstalks now brown,
bent and crinkly, crunching under hooves.

A telephone pole, stark, bare-boned, scarred—
another stalk in that dry field—loomed ahead.
She twitched the reins to the left, leaving lots of room,
began to canter, laughed at nothing but the joy of it.

I love it, she shouted. *Let's ride forever
and never come back.* But in the low sun's glare
she didn't, no, couldn't see the guy wire, the rusted
pole anchor stretching diagonally down.

Squinting, she turned to joke with Lucille.
The horse passed under, but the line caught her neck.
She hung there, for a moment weightless in that fall's
morning air, clung like a fruit not ready to drop.

No one heard the hollow thud
as the ground reached up to cradle her,
and for just a blink the world held its breath.
Nothing stirred, not one thing.

The Last Days

The Grateful Dead sing that the first days
are the hardest days. I'd say, naw, it's
the last ones: the goodbye, garbage days,
the gray ones. You know how it goes—
dissonance, lost lyrics, broken rhymes;
closing time with cranky pants
riding too low on the hips, cracks showing;
hope not even hanging on a thread,
dancers stepping on each other's toes.

All that splashed beer on the floor
sticky and screaming, "Party's over."
God, it's 2 a.m. and your plans are on the curb,
dreams in the gutter. What was promised
is piss in the wind, and your hoped-for-sex
a sodden fairy tale. The barkeep holds up cast-off
pipe dreams, wipes each clean with his dirty rag,
then stacks them neatly with all the others
he's stashed behind the bar.

The curtains hang limp, no breeze.
Nothing. Dancing's over, the juke box unplugged,
and the place stinks. Another Saturday night
down the tubes. Too soon you'll slope home alone
to your unmade bed. You wish it were different.
Don't you always? So you linger at the bar
with your silly grin, waiting for one last laugh,
one red sticky smile. Nothing. At the door you teeter,
eyes drooped and blinking, taking photos of footprints.

Different Tongues

It didn't start out as a day of learning when
a flock of fools—how apropos—found their way here:
a dodo, one flamingo, a lonely pelican toting eggs,
not to mention a trio of rare low-beaked gloaters.

These things happen in spite of best laid plans.
So I rolled up the hose, stopped my watering,
and welcomed them all, hoping for the best.
When fate flies in it's just better to let it be.

I offered water, some old amaranth seed,
an open-lawn policy, and we gathered—
warily, at first—for introductions and bobbing.
(I was surprised at how well it went.)

Then we settled into awkward small talk.
Speaking different tongues made it spongy,
but we soldiered on and I learned, I think,
that all were lost, no one really meaning to be here.

And as the afternoon stretched out over us,
a certain ease began to build, each finding
their spot: the dodo square to the porch corner,
the flamingo atop the rock sculpture.

The pelican had the hardest time finding purchase,
while the gloaters shined, plopping down wherever:
unconcerned with just right or almost perfect...
as if this was theirs, as if they were hosting.

I was most impressed, until, from the edge of my eye,
I saw the smallest give the tallest a half-hidden wink,
then follow up with a wily, slinky grin which
made me think, and finally wonder:

Who was fooling and who was being fooled?
that maybe there would be no happy ending
to this rare plume-filled serendipity, that perhaps
quick goodbyes and take-offs were looming.

So I ahem-ed, mumbled about the dark coming,
thanked them for dropping in, winked a friendly,
muttered, "Fly on back," but was sure to add,
"Next time call ahead. It's just what's right."

Nana Was a Seamstress

Nana was a seamstress.
"Like a window I open in the summer,"
she would say, her curled arthritic fingers
threading the needle's eye.

And I always wondered what she meant
'til I sat with her one stifling July night
and watched her smile, then slip away—
a breeze, her last clean and airy breath of light.

Nothing More

Our friend can't stop,
continues to vomit—
just bile now—
says she'll die tonight
and we know she's right.

She's keeps on shrinking
and pulling away, pushing off
like there's an opened door
which we can't see, around
some far-off corner.

We want to do more,
something, anything.
We ask. She shakes, "No."
So we hold her hands,
prop her up, wipe her brow.
It's the best we can do.

Look, she beams, *there,*
on the ceiling. Don't you...?
But we can't. *Tell us*, we whisper.
Her eyes close, then flicker.
A little gag. Nothing comes.
I have nothing left.

Six

Obituary

Clarence John Garret was born in Harristown on January 8, 1958, and passed this last Saturday, October 6, 2012. "Pawps," as he was called by everyone, labored all his working life at Placerton Feed. He could often be found at what he and his long time friends, Tom Henry, Sam Barrett, and Fairchild Dennis named "The Office," known to the rest of us as the Marshall Bar. Clarence was celebrated as "The Marshall of the Marshall," many times opening and closing the bar, sometimes sweeping up, oft-times swept out. Clarence was found early Monday morning comatose in Alley Three, blocks away from the Marshall and not far from the home he had shared with his estranged wife, Marla. "I guess he was headed here," she told this reporter, "though he knew I'd changed the locks. He was an habitual romantic who never understood the word 'no'." After the burial service at the Veterans Cemetery there will be a memorial to celebrate Pawp's life on Friday, October 12 at 3:00 pm in the Marshall Bar. As a tribute, donations to pay his bar tab will be appreciated.

A Good Job

In the circuses and parades
there is always some poor guy
walking behind the horses and the elephants,
downcast eyes, shoveling shit.

For sure it's important work
or else the marching bands and
baton twirlers, the clowns or
the Shriners, the unicyclists
might all end up...you know.

But telling that to his boy:
"Son, I'm the scooper-upper."
doesn't quite cut it, might
make him blush, even want to lie.

Better, to be a true scooper-upper—
show his son what real, honest work is—
men who'd follow us word bullshitters
with our lies and froth, our smirky smiles.

He'd show his boy his famous moves:
the pinched nose and knowing nod,
the sideways glance with looped half-grin,
the famous "bend and scoop" morphing
into the over-the-shoulder fling.

Armed with YouTube and backed by Twitter,
that's a job any man could be proud of.
And, think of the laughs, for sure the fame:
shiny footprints for his son to follow,
someday he a scooper-upper too.

Quiet

The lone wren sips from the birdbath
and the front yard mole's made three neat mounds.

A turkey vulture swoops by lazy, late-day-hunting,
while smoke-blue clouds roll away the hills.

The only sounds are the crickets, the wind,
a branch breaking, my own slow breathing.

Night skids in early now with new-found chill.
The wood is stacked and it's time to call it quits.

Best to heat up the stove, pour me some zin,
and slip into how much I miss my woman.

Ode To Birdie

If I were the pond I'd sport her some ripples,
invite in the wind and offer up fish,
who'd jump as an offering into the boat.

And if I were that boat I'd do a slow trip
'round the pond, ask that shy mallard afloat
in the reeds to join and make a parade.

If I were the wildflowers I'd outlast the season,
be extra bright and wave in the breeze,
be super saucy, flirt with her spirit.

And if I were her man coming back from the hunt
I'd pretend she was there, bring better stories,
big hunger too, lie a bit, and clean up after.

If I were that raven I'd soar with her up
over Sawtooth Hill, then swoop down to clutch
memories, wisdom, fat scraps of love.

But because I'm her friend I'll build her a shrine.
I'll go there to visit from time to time,
plant her some roses—red ones, I think.

Then let Birdie know that her no-nonsense,
her home-spun, gifted me full, tell her
death is a comma, that I'll see her again

Listening to Satellite Radio

Listening to satellite radio,
the station: "Heart and Soul,"
some bluesy, jazzy guy sings
about "Loving your pretty wings," which,
I guess, is a metaphor for legs or arms.

So I'm curious what my wife would say
if I came upon her in the kitchen
and mentioned that I love her foxy wings.
Since the silky guy sings it sexy
I wonder, too, what if I breathed that softly
in our bedroom while making love.

I see her grin, get all-a-tingle, my finally noticing,
then unfurl those satin feathers, spread them,
and slowly lift up from our bed,
her pretty wings—like an angel's—
soundlessly, simply, whisking her off,
leaving me filled with longing and awe,
with one wild, divine dose of envy.

Our Trip to the Sea

"One day you'll be a lampoon," she clapped,
"You know, a *New Yorker* cartoon:
  an old man sitting in a corner
  at the nursing home, his trusty cane
  lifting up the skirt of his caretaker."

I laughed, "What's the caption?"
"Something like, 'Nurse Cochran,
  I've misplaced my catheter.' "
"That's not even funny," I said. "Come on,"
  she shot back, "Not bad for off the cuff."

The car crapped out in Carpenteria,
  so we hitched, then hiked to some hidden cove,
  where we pitched the tent and set up camp.
"So, what's this comic, Ms. Cleverpuss?"
"Ah," she said, "'Unexpected Consequences.'"

Then, after a dinner of hummus and carrots:
"Mmmm," she said, "I'd sure like a cappuccino."
"How about some slow kissing," I clowned.
"Maybe, sure, but what's the caption?"
"I know: 'First stop on the road to cloning.'"

"Pretty good, my dear, for off the cuff."
  I put my arm out, she snuggled in close
  and we counted gulls, named clouds
  as they scuttled dark off the coast.
  She had the best one: Giant's Cudgel.

Night came fast and with no fire it got way cold,
  so we crawled in our bags, Houdini-ed from our clothes.
  We were quiet, holding hands, just us and the sea.
  I thought, "I love our love," that it needed a caption.
  It was sappy, but I liked it: "Real, not cartoons."

Waiting For the Rapture

Sitting at the holy grounds
my shirt starched and pressed,
my knees bouncing to head-tunes,
my crown tarnished and askew,
I am waiting for the Rapture.

Needing my shoes to shine
I've slapped on some salad dressing—
Mrs. Renfro's, if you want to know.
Sparkle they do, smiling back at me
while we're waiting for the Rapture.

I got good old Ray in my ear buds
letting me know it's gonna be all right,
and since there are no cosmic accidents,
I know we're both onto something
us two waiting for the Rapture.

The three motorcycle cops vroom-vroom by,
their calf-high, black boots sparkling,
their sunglasses mirroring me all a-smile,
and they nod-nod-nod, the best they can do
as they're heading for the Rapture.

I sip my sixth cup of bad news coffee,
knees bouncing with caffeine-hope and sneaky glee,
as my bleached-blond neighbor with the hourglass bod
nods my way, slips downhill, sashays slinky,
punching her ticket for the Rapture.

Here I am sitting tall, all agleam, grinning like a fool,
making up how it's gonna be: me and that harpy host of angels;
the Big Guy on his golden throne, his white beard flowing.
Everyone is smiling. We pat each others' backs,
tip our hats when we pass, all lolling and strolling in the Rapture.

About The Author

Because he loves to, Russ Messing has been writing for much of his one wild and loving life. He has written mainly for himself—journals, stories, and poetry—and has self-published two books of Haiku—one haiku a day for two different years. He was a high school Spanish teacher in St. Louis and is co-founder of Synergy Elementary School in San Francisco. He is a psychologist, makes award-winning olive oil, and lives in a small slice of heaven outside of Healdsburg, CA.